# Cries From Quarantine

### POEMS ABOUT LOVE

# ACKNOWLEDGMENTS

# BECAUSE OF YOU

Gratitude and blessings to my beautiful friends and family.

You have my back and therefore I AM and I CAN.

To my special friend: thank you for seeing me. What a wonderfully strange bond we've enjoyed. Living life with more compassion, patience, acceptance and understanding are results of knowing and loving you.

For all the fearful lovers: you'll grow out of that uncertainty the more you fall in love with yourself. Let people love you the way they know how.

What do you have to lose but love?

*Cries From Quarantine*

Dana N. Anderson

# WHY LOVE

# ANGRY LOVE

# UNCONDITIONAL LOVE

# SELF LOVE

# FOREWORD

# Things I learned about love

When love found me, I thought I was ready.

Then I got extremely uncomfortable

with love's imperfect way

and pushy persistence.

When love found me, he was not my "type." He just possessed so many qualities that I could appreciate, both positive and negative. He spoke to me with love. This is because he saw me exactly as I was. Raw, flawed, beautiful, nurturing, soft and resilient. He recognized I knew pain yet he SAW me as love.

I only knew one way. When a relationship felt too uncertain, I would let Ego take over every fiber of my being and do her best to get rid of the discomfort.

(Not without playing the victim, of course.)

This love was gooooood. Every opportunity I found to run away from him, he stopped Ego in her tracks. This love understood he was not perfect but more than anything he was not going to let me throw love away. This one was different. He was not moved by my fiery temper and sharp tongue. In fact, I believe he was completely in tune with the words that I could not say. I LOVED HIM. But I was afraid to get hurt again. My heart cried, "KEEP YOUR DISTANCE."

So there I was, exposed and vulnerable, "stuck" in a way that I was struggling to embrace. This love was not familiar, not physically close and came from a world to which I held a serious side eye. I had no idea what to do. Sometimes I'd try to go with the flow; sometimes I'd try to kill him dead. Nothing worked. Why the hell did I attract this?!

I started writing to cope with some of these uncomfortable, deep feelings. Poetry became more and more of an outlet. Not since high school had I written this way. I started to refer to this collection as "things I learned about love" and took the scary step of starting to share these poems. First to friends, then on Instagram.

The love was still around but the relationship would fade in and out. I just wanted to get rid of him! Hard to get someone out of your heart and life when they still have things to teach you about yourself. I even suppressed my desire to write about love—in any form—and looked away from the collection.

Then Covid-19. The pandemic. The quarantine. What does a creative do in isolation? Go within. Suddenly I was overcome with the desire to not just share my poems but to hear them in my voice. To explore my deep connection with this love and surrender. Finally.

As I played with the words, I gained a sense of freedom. My eyes were opening up to who I am and what I want. No coincidence that one day as I was scrolling through social media I came across my friend Greg's painting. Not only did I not know he was that kind of artist but I also didn't imagine that a piece of visual art would inspire my work.

That's the book cover. That's it! The subject of "Pandemic Painting" was me: a strong woman, yet fragile. Poised and present. Content in solitude. Intriguing and still seeking. In quarantine, she turns her eyes within and finds her voice.

*Cries From Quarantine* has been a long time in the making. Reflections about love of all kinds, shared from the soul. I hope you find yourself in these things I learned about love.

Love is persistent.

Don't try to resist it.

Sometimes you don't know what love is.

# WHY LOVE

# UNTITLED

Intense

Confident

Illuminating

Defining

Life-giving

Affirming

All in the way he looks at ME.

# HOWWW???

How does he do that to me
How does he know
The thought of him touching me
My heart explodes
Ain't even sexually
It's just the flow
That instantaneous feeling
It's love fa sho

How did he smell this on me
How did he know
That I need intensity
Not just a show
A connectivity like—it's magical
An electricity surge
So powerful

How does he do this to me
Ain't like he tries
It's just his energy type
Turns other guys
Into a cold memory
That quickly dies
The minute he looks at me
Deep in my eyes

My head keeps spinning
I can't believe it all
For now I soak his love in
I just let go.

# NO WORDS

Eyes say what we don't
Tongue down my throat
Squeeze my jaw but it won't hurt
Breathe so hard I can't hear
Leg pressed against my ear
Hand inside my thigh
Nibbling from my toes down to
My slip n slide
Grips along my side
Escape as I let out a sigh
A moan
I'm not in this alone...
Cuz it's just what we do


Make   me   want   ~~to fuck~~ you

# LOVE IS

Love is imperfect
Inconvenient
Never on time—
Yet right on time

Love is purifying
Dramatically divine
Radically consuming—
The life-altering kind

Love isn't easy
Until you love you
It can make or break you
Turn you into a complete fool

We have an abundance
Love wants to overflow
Latch right on to you
Never let go

Always within
Never without
Choose to see it
Choose to be it

We are love
At our core
What we want
Is a little more

Of the sometimes sweet
Sometimes bitter
Make us better
Forever kind of love.

# UNCONDITIONAL LOVE

# THEY AIN'T PERFECT BUT...

Thank God for brothers
I love black men
Glad they walk this planet
So I can
Give them
Long squeezes
Tight hugs
A lot of sass
Tough love
Smart mouth
Good grub
Shiiieeettt...
I'll even hold his hand
My full attention
My best advice
The fun parts of me
(Ya know...)
When they treat me nice.

## ROSE QUARTZ

I want to
Wash your pain away
Heal those wounds with love
Wipe away
Your tears
Send you light from above
I want to be
The One
With whom
You share
Your fears
I'll tell you
You were brave
All those
complicated years
Give you laughter
Where there is tension
Give you praise
Where there's been no mention

Hand you intimacy
With no intention
I'll let you be your own invention
We can have
A beautiful life of our design
Me and You
In our own time
More love
More patience
Walk to our own cadence
When we are healed and whole
Our Love
Will be unstoppable.

# PLACES

Train tracks
Freight cars
I was walking real far
Just to get away
From how bright I shined
A true star

Sunset
Moon rise
They say it's full
It's all lies
'Cause I feel nothing inside
Empty as your cold eyes

June heat
Sweaty thighs
I feel nice so I sigh
But you're not here
I realize
I'm all alone with my high

Lush trees
Hike trail
I was searching for a spell
Just to break a way
From how you pull me into
Your hell

What happened to our soul ties?
What happened to that love tide?
The wave that crashed my Heart
And had me drowning in you

What happened to our soul ties?
What happened to that love high?
I'm calling in a lifeline
Just to save me and you

Full moon
Sun rise
A whole new day
So I'll try
To fill the void and get by
Do everything that comes to mind

Fall crisp
Inner thrill
I feel frisky so I will
Act like you're here
With me still
I'm all alone I have free will

Twilight
Bright stars
Saw you in your big car
Flashin by with some broad
Said peace by with ya
Wasn't hard

Beach front
High tide
Wash away my tears inside
Feel so free that my vibe
Is so at peace
I might fly.

# FOR THE WIN

Just when you think it's dead
That spark ignites all over again
As you play out the game in your head
Hope comes and goes
You'll struggle within

This is only a means to an end
Each day is unique
Deep in your heart nothing's changed
Feelings come and go
But you'll begin

To challenge the joy
The euphoria
The connection
The blissful dreams you spin

The question is
Will you give up
Let go
Be yourself
Hold on
Have faith
Give in to the fear
Who claims the win?

When it's
You versus LOVE
May the only casualty be
The ego you wrestle
And pin.

# CHOSEN LOVE

Family is
The thread
The fabric
That builds
The patchwork quilt
Warm, tattered
That always covers and protects
All of us
Who share the same story
And the same love
Doesn't mean the same blood.

# GOODNIGHT

I would have planned goodbye
I would have wished you well
I didn't realize how quickly time
Moves swiftly when you fail
To say the meaningful and meaningless words
That keep us feeling swell
A call
A card
A visit
That smile when you answered your doorbell
We laughed about the past
Celebrated the present
Wanted you to approve my future
You had to bless my suitor
I loved how you believed in me
I'll keep that in my heart
Let that be a reminder
Plant a seed
When I'm feeling dark
I know life is a cycle
Of beginnings and ends
Leaving us was inevitable
You were truly a Godsend.

# GROWN UP LOVE

I made a choice

I was deliberate

I wanted a liberating kind of love

That was my voice

From deep within

Setting me free to give away my love

Yes that felt strange

All I've known is pain

Now there's no conditions on my love

Close my eyes tight

See my heart's sights

Living in a dream with all this love

Perfect it's not

Ain't what I thought

Yet I've embraced this way of love

Keep my mind clear

Tongue's not a spear

And I give thanks—finally, pure love.

# WE

We would have been unstoppable
Nothing in this world could have broken us
WE would have made our mark on love
Showed the world something remarkable

Somehow WE let things fall apart
Bridge crumbled right between us
I reached out to catch your fingertips
Space and time beat we, the lovestruck

I still see all the good in you
Do you still see deep in my heart?
Within there's a reflection of you
A shining spirit, healed, unscarred

Oh don't mind me
I'm just grieving you
Dare I say US?
Or is it WE?

I dream of YOU
There's still an US
My soul still whispers
WE.

I've let you go
But hold you close
When I lie
Comfortably

I dream of YOU
There's still an US
My soul still whispers
WE.

# ANGRY LOVE

# I HATE YOU

I hate you
I said it
I will live to regret it
I'm leaving
You're dead
You won't fuck with my head
I'm angry
You're wrong
Go write your little songs
I hate you
Not sad
I hope you're doing bad.

# RHODIUM

Stop telling me that I'm strong
Just so you can be weak
Instead of building me up
Climb your own mountain peak
Be loyal to yourself
I'll stay loyal to me
When I see you're ready
Then you + I can be we
Patient I've never been
Yet I'm trying to stay true
Stop telling me that I'm strong
Just so you can stay YOU.

# YOUR MISTAKE

(The Thirst Trap Rap)

Another fake out
I had to break out
N***** will play you
For a hoe who just
Chase clout
The wannabe models
Who can't afford bottles
Phony career bios
Fake goals to follow

...Yeah I bit the bait
Now I sit back and wait
Watchin you lookin lame
I call it your fate

Bro, you ATE the bait
Now I sit back and wait
Cringing, damn you look lame
Watchin' a broken man's fate

You thought you were doing something
Now you're glued to a trap
Bet you prayed that the DM gods would
Take that thirst quench back

Hope the sex was really really good
Better yet kinky GR8
That is if she's giving you some...
Heard she's still taking dates
Does that baby look JUST like you?
Lemme stop with this hate
I mean I get to laugh at you
Watch me glow—
YOUR MISTAKE.

You might call it angst
And try to escape
Run away from the pain you caused
With your lies
Your mistake

You might call this a waste
Say that I've gone insane
Run away from the pain you caused
Narcissist on the take.

# BRIGHT SIDE

I'm on the bright side of the moon
Everything I claim is true

What's good for us over here
Is not the living truth for you

I'm on the right side of the trial
My testimony is worthwhile

I'm cleaning up my mess
Peace out
I'm moving on
I needed to confess
Without a shout
I dropped a bomb

This isn't just a test
I've had enough
That's why I'm calm
You wanted to have the best
Then took the bait
And broke the bond

Glued your life to a trap
I can't respect
So now I'm wrong
I'll stop beating you up
The fight is stale
Last punch, I'm done

We can't be what we were
Can you accept
The trust is gone
The next time you see me
Kiss my sweet ass
And watch   your   tone

# THE EXPERT

Making me feel wonderful
Was just your specialty
You living in the moment
Felt so authentic to me
Whispering to my soul
That's just your specialty
Reflections of my mind
You work so craftily

And when the shift came in
I knew that drift would win
Took my heart for a spin
I'm fooled by love again

Making me feel high
That was your specialty
You trying SO hard
Really came effortlessly

Lighting up my smile
That's just your specialty
Planting seeds of hope
Done so intelligently

But when the shift came in
I knew this drift would win
Took my heart for a spin
I'm fooled by love again
Sir, you've done fine work
I caved in—my heart, my knees
Drumroll please...
Give it up...for The Expert

# SELF LOVE

# GIVE MY HEART BACK TO ME

I don't feel safe anymore
Since you walked out that door
Too much time has passed
Thought our magic could last
Can't blame you for this
Set myself up for a hard hit
I've seen this before
Red flags I won't ignore
Drifting far away from me
Into a flashy world where we
Can't exist as one
Dreams of you once were fun
Now thoughts I must control
Space finally took its toll
Slipped my armor back on
Told myself I'm done
What I learned this time
Will stay on my mind
My heart ain't a place
Men use to escape

Give my heart back to me
Leave it where you found it
Go seek your new prey
Please just stay away

Bring my heart back here
But don't stand too near
Go find beautiful prey
Please just stay away

Put my heart where it was
But don't stay because
That space still feels weak
Let me be complete

# THE BOUNCEBACK

I'm not okay
But I'll be fine
That part of me
I've left behind

Not over it yet
But I will be
Soon as I wipe
My memory

Outdone I was
Now I'm just numb
Going through the motions
Mind on the run

I'm not okay
But I'll be fine
I'm like the Phoenix
Watch my flame shine.

# KEEPING BUSY

Got my girls
We rock worlds
With a flirty smirk I twirl
My hair's done got lotsa curls
Baby, I'm just keeping busy
Make this look easy when I'm busy

Struttin round
Getting down
Smiling at new boys in town
Won't catch me out with a frown
Baby I'm keeping busy
I'm better when I'm busy

Hit a lick
He moves quick
Took me on a shopping trip
Don't worry he don't mean sh**
That's just the way I'm
keeping busy
I'm smiling when I'm busy

So much fun
Made me c***
Dancing like I'm drunk off rum
This ain't a game, you're still the one
My heart's not done, I am simply keeping busy
You know you love me when I'm busy.

# S.O.S.

I need The Negotiator
Hostage situation underway
Narcissist snatched my heart
Says forever he'll stay

No I didn't invite him
He's got my neck yoked up
Sick part is that I love him
This has me all choked up

Can you call in the pros
I need someone who's tough
To take this shrewd man down
I know I'm not strong enough

Free my heart from this episode
An action flick that won't end
Understand this is crisis mode
I beg of you, please defend

Send over a sharpshooter
To loosen this warlock's grip
To pull me out of this torture
But promise me you won't kill him
Just save me first, move me forward.

# WHAT'S YOURS IS MINE?

(By a Fragile Girl Who Fell for a Delightfully F*cked Up Boy)

My tears are your tears
But your tears aren't mine
Before your sweet
whispers
My whole life was fine

I was in love with me
My life was complete
Before you stepped in
And changed up my heartbeat

My fears are your fears
But your fears aren't mine
Before your sweet whispers
My life was on time

My days had a rhythm
My nights were noise free
Before you snuck in
With a slick melody

What's mine is yours...
What's yours ain't mine...
What's mine is yours
But that ain't fine

What's mine is yours
And now I'm tired
What's mine ain't yours
So I...so I draw the line

My needs are your needs
But your needs aren't mine
Before your sweet
nothings
My boundaries could bind

I had my neat files
My cold heart tucked away
Before you peeked in
And learned just the right play

My issues belong to me
Yours were much worse
Now I'm stuck on stupid
So your name I curse

My issues belong to me
But you made yours mine
Now I'm stuck on stupid...
So I...I wrote you this rhyme.

What's mine is yours...
What's yours ain't mine...
What's mine is yours
But that ain't fine

What's mine is yours
But now I'm tired
What's mine ain't yours
So I'm taking back...taking back my time

# SUPER MOON SPELLBREAK

Spellbound no more
I've left heartache behind
Disappearing acts
Soul sucking vibes
One-sided supply
(I'll consider them a gift in kind)

Thank you for your service
You've taught me loads about me
How much value I have, I'm a GODDESS!
You certainly couldn't resist me.

Grateful for your wizardry
For I must have been in a haze
To let your words convince me
My heart needed to stay

Jailbreak goes my heart
Free from that binding spell
Soaring on to new heights
Distant from your personal hell

I wish you only peace
I trust you'll find it soon
I'm sure you don't believe me
But I'm under my own love spell now,
You FOOL.

CPSIA information can be obtained
at www.ICGtesting.com
Printed in the USA
BVHW030930080421
604475BV00007B/1022

9 780578 786544